Published in 2021 by Rob Sawyer/1878 Books

Copyright 2021 Rob Sawyer

ISBN: 978-1-7399392-0-5

Design and typesetting by Thomas Regan - Milkyone Creative
Front cover image of Keith by Kyle Mainwaring

DEDICATION
In memory of Henry Sanderson, my grandfather
and Blackburn Rovers supporter.

CONTENTS

INTRODUCTION

Keith Newton helped to define the blueprint for the modern full-back. He was a natural athlete; fast, strong in the tackle, assured on the ball and always looking to bomb forward on the overlap to deliver pinpoint crosses.

In over a decade at Ewood Park, the Mancunian developed into a highly sought-after internationally capped player, capable of operating with assurance on either flank. The move to trophy-chasing Everton – dubbed the School of Science – in late 1969 should have been a match made in football heaven. Seen as the Toffees' long-term successor to World Cup-winner Ray Wilson, Keith earned a League Championship medal and excelled for England at the 1970 World Cup finals in Mexico. And yet, he endured a largely frustrating spell on Merseyside, leaving without fanfare on a free transfer when his contract expired in 1972.

He had the satisfaction of proving his doubters at Everton wrong by excelling and rediscovering his passion for the game in six happy seasons with Burnley thus becoming one of the few footballers to be held in high esteem by supporters on either side of the East Lancashire divide. After a spell in non-League football, he stepped away from the game, running a shop and working in sales in the motor trade.

Keith passed away in 1998 - taken at just 56 by cancer. He is fondly remembered by many as a brilliant player and supremely likeable person. This is his story.

CHAPTER ONE
A MANCHESTER LAD

Keith Robert Newton was born on 23 June 1941, to parents Robert and Amelia (Milly), and raised in Abbey Hey, Gorton, to the east of central Manchester. Robert was an ex-Royal Marine who had seen action at Dunkirk in 1940, and went on to work at a brick factory. He was just 57 when he passed away in 1960.

The Newton family was of the Manchester City persuasion and Keith and his brother Derek (the elder sibling by eight years) were always keen footballers. Both would play for hours on the nearby Mellands playing fields. If Keith was fouled, his big brother would see to it that the aggressor would not transgress again. Milly subsequently would declare – always out of Keith's earshot - that Derek was the more naturally talented player. Maybe this was true, but a bout of tuberculosis, and a prolonged spell recuperating at a sanatorium near Abergele, saw Derek let go by Manchester City after a couple of seasons in the youth team. Instead, he had become a plumber - probably earning more than he would have done as a footballer in that era.

Growing up, Keith played as an inside-forward for his school team - a factor in him being so comfortable on the ball and confident going forward once he switched to more defensive roles. Having impressed playing for Didsbury Technical School, Ryder Brow Boys Club and Spurley Hey Youth Club he was selected for the Reddish Senior Inter-League representative side (1955/56). Selection for Manchester Schoolboys B team brought the forward to the attention of Bolton

Keith, seated second from left, in a local youth team circa 1953

Reddish Senior Inter-League team 1955-56 season - Keith is fourth from left

Wanderers, but his trial as an amateur with the Trotters proved to be short and unsuccessful.

Therefore, Keith was obliged to start working in a Mancunian mill. He would claim that the monotony of watching the precision grinder do its job for 20 minutes after he had set it up, drove him to open his first packet of cigarettes. Although Keith would go on to regret his smoking habit, he didn't think that it affected his sporting performance. When interviewed at his home in 1967, he was observed by the journalist Geoffrey Rumney to be a nervous smoker: 'Forever taking the ash off the end by twirling the cigarette round in the middle of the ash tray.' This habit is reminiscent of his erstwhile Rovers colleague, Roy Vernon — another character who was comfortable in his skin, yet chain smoked heavily as a seemingly nervous habit.

CHAPTER TWO
THE CAREY CHICK

The 16-year-old was rescued from factory life in 'Cottonopolis' when he was spotted playing local football by Blackburn Rovers' scout Eric Walker. The courtship by Rovers' supremo Johnny Carey proved to be persuasive and the forward signed amateur forms in March 1958. Cutting his teeth as a manager at Ewood Park, the Irishman had gained a reputation for signing and nurturing young talent and blending it with experienced pros. His so-called 'Carey's Chicks' side - boasting Ronnie Clayton, Bryan Douglas, Ally MacLeod and Roy Vernon in the ranks - was thrilling to watch and restored top flight status to Rovers in 1958.

Coming through at youth level was a golden generation for the club. Developing in the 'colts' alongside Keith were fellow future international players Fred Pickering (at this point deployed at left-back) and Mike England. By the time Keith turned professional, six months after joining, Carey was on the point of departing Blackburn to manage Everton. Keith would prove to be the manager's fine parting gift for his successor, Dally Duncan, and the Rovers board.

Keith's daily rail commute from Gorton to East Lancashire necessitated a connection being made in central Manchester. During the layover between trains, he would grab a coffee in a café along with several other young Mancunian Rovers players, including Paddy Daly (his future best man) and Sandy Busby (son of the Manchester United manager). It was here that he first met Barbara Marsden. Bury-raised, where she had watched matches at Gigg Lane with her father, Barbara had become an ardent Manchester United supporter after the family moved to Sale. She was working as a secretary for the Rank Film Organisation on Deansgate, and with her friends would frequent the same cafe as the aspiring footballers. Although she was not initially smitten with Keith, romance would blossom in time. But first he had to get his hairstyle changed from one described in an article as 'fair hair standing up all round his head like a field of shaved corn'. This look earned him the nickname 'Bopper' – which eventually morphed into 'Bunny'. Once dating, the couple would become known as 'Bunny and Babs'.

In the 1958/59 FA Youth Cup competition, Rovers Colts, coached by Jackie Campbell, beat Newcastle United and Portsmouth to advance to a two-legged semi-final tie with Manchester United. Having drawn 1-1 at Ewood Park, Rovers stunned the 35,000 crowd at a floodlit Old Trafford by winning 3-2 on the night, and 4-3 on aggregate. The match was a personal triumph for Keith. Switched from inside-forward to centre-half due to an injury to Trevor Rimmer, he excelled. A match report singled out the 'lofty Newton' for praise: 'Superb in the air, he refused to be ruffled even at full stretch and, quite rightly, always played for safety.' At left-half in the youth side was Vinnie Leech. He'd make an interesting comparison between his Rovers teammate and another future England international player who he played with later in his career at Bury: 'You'd think that Keith and Colin Bell were twins. They were exactly the same in stature: they had long legs and speed. Both could do at bit of everything.'

In the Youth Cup final, Rovers met a West Ham team boasting future World Cup stars Geoff Hurst and Bobby Moore. The first leg, at Upton Park, ended with the honours even, 1-1. The return match at Ewood Park was similarly tight. Keith's form as a commanding stand-in centre-half, keeping West Ham's Mike Beesley in check, was described as a 'revelation' in one match report. Barry Griffiths had pulled off a tremendous save from a Hammers spot kick to keep Rovers on level-pegging. Finally, the deadlock was broken in Rovers' favour by Paddy Daly, with nine minutes of extra time remaining. Rovers clung on for a sweet victory and captain Fred Pickering was presented with the highly prized trophy by Sir Stanley Rous - Secretary of the Football Association.

Blackburn Rovers - FA Youth Cup Winners 1959. Keith is on back row, thrid from right

Subsequently, a celebration event was arranged at the Blackburn Public Halls by the Rovers Supporters Club. Here the silverware was presented, once more, to Fred Pickering by local MP Barbara Castle, with the Mayor and Mayoress of the town watching on. A few years ago, Mike England reflected on the great achievement for the *Lancashire Telegraph*: 'We were just young players and we played against all the big clubs. We were watched by 36,000 at Manchester United in the semi-final. There was a hell of a crowd at Blackburn Rovers for the final as well. We had never seen crowds like it. It really was an incredible experience and I still remember it now, even after everything else I experienced in football. It was a very special time and several of those players went on to become very good professionals. It doesn't happen often that three or four of your team go on to become internationals for their countries and, when I look back now, I have no doubts that I have Blackburn Rovers to thank for helping me in my career.'

Following a summer break, the youth team headed to Sanremo on the Italian

Riviera to take part in the Torneo Internazionale Carlin's Boys. The invitational under-19s event, organised by local amateur club AS Carlin's Boys, was in its twelfth year. Having breezed past Swiss opponents Vevey Sports in the opening group match, Rovers squeezed past the hosts (1-0) to confirm a semi-final place against FC Barcelona. In this fixture Paddy Daly scored for Rovers but two goals in reply saw the Catalans through to the final, which they won. Rovers contested a third-place play-off against Internazionale of Milan - losing 2-0.

Keith's elevation to the Rovers first team came a year later when, at the age of 19, he deputised at left-half for the injured Michael McGrath. It was no gentle introduction as the visitors were Tommy Docherty's Chelsea - and facing Keith was Jimmy Greaves, who was already capped by England. Inspired by Bryan Douglas' prompting at inside-left, plus the firepower of Peter Dobing and Derek Dougan, Rovers stormed to a 3-1 victory. The debutant came out well in his personal duel with Greaves. The *Lancashire Telegraph* reported: 'Young Newton certainly did not let Rovers down. Like all the Rovers wing-halves he likes to attack, but he stuck grimly to Greaves and the Chelsea man was certainly not the force he was in the first meeting of the teams at Stamford Bridge.' His second outing was in a defeat to Preston after which he found himself back in the reserves. Just shy of six feet tall, Keith was well-suited to the centre-half role but Mike England's dominance in the defensive pivot role, having switched from wing-half, severely restricted Keith's opportunities there. Having struggled to establish himself in the team, thoughts had turned to a life outside football and Keith started looking for jobs in Manchester. However, he persevered and settled, helped by his courtship with Barbara.

After left-back Dave Whelan broke his leg in the 1960 FA Cup final, former England international Bill Eckersley was recalled to the team. Subsequently Fred Pickering and John Bray were tried in the position without totally convincing. Jack Marshall, who had replaced Dally Duncan as manager, gave Keith a run at left-back in the reserves in March 1961 and was impressed enough to promote the Mancunian to the first team in that position for the final six matches of the season. Fred Pickering, meanwhile, switched to centre-forward with devastating effect.

Blackburn Rovers and Barcelona youth teams in Sanremo in 1959

Keith would go on to spend extended periods of his club career on the left side of defence, in spite of being naturally right-footed - a testament to his ability and versatility. Footage from the full-back's time at Everton shows him confidently delivering crosses and free-kicks with his, supposedly weaker, left foot. Jack Marshall would comment, 'You can play Keith anywhere in defence - right, left or centre-half - and he'll look right at home.' England star and Rovers teammate Bryan Douglas was another impressed with Keith's emergence and development in the back line: 'He'd been quite an ordinary inside-right but as a full-back he came on a ton. He grew in confidence and stature.' A young fan in this era getting an early glimpse of Keith was Mike Jackman – who'd go on to become a Rovers historian. One recollection was of how close children could get to their sporting heroes – even running errands for them: 'I remember as a kid in the early 1960s they had a cinder car park by the ground that they trained on. We'd go down and watch them. Keith was a smoker - as most of the players were. There was this little hut there and any number of the players would be in it smoking. When we were getting their autographs, they'd send us across to the shop to get their cigarettes.'

CHAPTER THREE
WEDDING BELLS
AND ENGLAND HOPES

On the romantic front, a clandestine courtship had been going on. Barbara would tell her parents that she was going to Manchester with her girlfriends - but on the bus she'd apply her make-up and meet Keith at a dancehall. Wedding bells had been delayed by the reticence of Barbara's father, James, to give his daughter's hand in marriage to a 'flashy footballer' (a misplaced apprehension - Keith was far removed from this stereotype). The engagement ring gathered dust in Barbara's bedroom until Keith plucked up courage to ask James for permission a second time, having turned 21 in June 1962. Barbara's mother had a quiet word with her husband and, this time, he gave his blessing. On 15 June 1963, the couple tied the knot at the Unitarian Church in Bury. Many Blackburn Rovers players were in attendance at the nuptials. Bryan Douglas was snapped for the local newspaper giving the bride a congratulatory peck on the cheek.

The marriage was a true partnership of equals. Barbara, who had changed her football allegiance to Blackburn Rovers, become a great – often forthright – cheerleader for her modest and easy-going husband. In an era before agents, she was always there to act as a sounding board for him and would speak out publicly on his behalf, if it was deemed necessary. Asked early in 1968 what life was like as the wife of a famous footballer, she disclosed that the most difficult part was being alone for prolonged periods: 'Keith is away every other weekend and being an international doesn't help matters much. At the beginning, you don't mind so

1963 - Barbara gets a peck on the check from Bryan Douglas, as the groom looks on

much, but by the end of the season you really get fed up. We hardly ever get out together now – especially since the arrival eight weeks ago of baby Craig.'

The newlyweds honeymooned in Newquay before settling into married life in a semi-detached house on Langdale Close, Feniscowles. The road gained the nickname 'The Rovers Reserve' as half a dozen players lived there. Keith's nephew, David, vividly recalls visiting his uncle's home and being starstruck by the likes of Fred Pickering and Ronnie Clayton popping in for a chat. A few years later the couple moved with their young son, Craig, to Wilpshire on the outskirts of Blackburn.

Local lad Mick Thexton recalls how accessible Keith and his contemporaries were in the 1960s, compared to nowadays: 'Keith lived in a club house next door to Billy Wilson, the other Rovers full-back. My gran and grandad lived opposite, and we used to always visit them en route to the match. I have memories of kicking a ball in the street with Keith and Billy on a Saturday morning – I would sit on my ball at the end of Gran and Grandad's drive, waiting for them to come out to go down to Ewood. It was hardly a full training session – just a few passes back and forth across the road! A few years later, my grandparents liked to go on cruises and planned for months in advance for the cruise fancy dress competition. Keith lent them his full England kit (including boots) so that my grandad could go as "World Cup Willie".'

Two years after her wedding day, Barbara took her parents to Wembley to watch Keith's senior England debut. With the teams lined up in readiness to be introduced to Princess Alexandra, and the National Anthem being played, James visibly welled-up with emotion. When Barbara enquired what the matter was, he responded: 'There's 11 England players on the pitch, and one of them is ours.' Barbara was quick to quip back: 'Yes, but he wasn't one of ours two years ago, was he Daddy?' James had come to accept Keith for the good husband that he was. From then on, he rivalled Barbara as biggest supporter of Keith's playing career, following him to most of his matches and, with his wife, giving him a gift every time he earned an England cap.

Prior to the late 1950s, full-backs had essentially been there to protect their goal, and little else. Standing sentinel in their own half, crossing the half-way line to join in the attack was an anathema to many. With the evolution from the long-established W-M formation, full-backs had more licence and inclination to link up with the forwards. Roger Byrne at Manchester United (before his passing in Munich in 1958), Alex Parker at Everton, Jim Langley and George Cohen of Fulham and Jimmy Armfield at Blackpool are some examples of the new breed – but it's arguable that Keith took the concept of an attacking full-back to a new level due to his unrivalled athleticism combined with all-round ability.

For Fred Cumpstey, a long-standing Rovers fanatic, watching Keith develop into the doyen of full-backs was a joy: 'Keith is unchallenged in my opinion as the best right full-back I've seen in a blue and white shirt. It was his sheer athleticism which set Newton apart from others. He was arguably the first of the attacking full backs gifted with abundant and dynamic energy, plus powers of recovery that were second to none. His positional sense enabled him to be in the right place at the right time. This, harnessed to his economy of effort and letting the ball do the work, rendered him the classiest of footballers. A consummate professional, a high-octane player with a silky touch and as classy a footballer as you could ever wish to see; he is in my all-time best Rovers XI.'

One player Keith struck up an understanding with on the left side of the Rovers formation in the mid-1960s was Michael McGrath – the team's Irish international left-half. For McGrath, it was a very fruitful partnership: 'A classy player, Keith was a joy to play alongside. I would do a bit of the donkey work and he would go forward beyond me - he could overlap and cross the ball. Also, he wasn't frightened of coming inside and having a whack at goal - being right-footed comes in handy if you want to come inside from the left and have a clear shot at goal.'

England Under 23 team in Budapest 13 May 1964. Keith is third from left. John Talbut, next to Terry Venables, captains the side. Keith scored an own goal but England won 2-1

Assured performances at club level caught the attention of the England set-up, but Keith's international career was initially beset by ill-fortune. His England Under 23 debut in February 1964 - a 3-2 victory over Scotland in which Fred Pickering grabbed a hat-trick - was followed by an immediate invitation to join

*Fred Pickering congratutales
Keith at his home on his first
England Under 23 call-up.
Barbara looks on*

*Keith looking pensive,
around 1964*

18

1966 in Glasgow with England manager Alf Ramsey

a senior squad training camp at Lea Green, near Matlock. It was curtailed for Keith when he damaged a cartilage in a practice match collision with Birmingham City's Mike Hellawell on a slippery pitch. One of Keith's legs got trapped under the other and he felt a tell-tale stab of pain in his knee. Returning to Lancashire for assessment by a specialist, he said: 'It is a terrible blow. I was looking forward to getting to Wembley with Blackburn. I was also looking forward to winning more Under 23 caps.'

The injury necessitated the removal of cartilage from his left knee in a Manchester hospital, where he had Manchester United's Noel Cantwell for company in the adjacent bed. Although there were hopes that he'd be playing again in late March, Keith missed all but the last match of the domestic season (by which point Rovers' title hopes had ebbed away). The recovery was just in time for him to go on the England Under 23's tour of Europe in the close season.

In February 1965 the full-back had to drop out of a three-day England training camp, held at Lilleshall in Shropshire, after injuring his ankle in a match at Filbert Street. He was out for six weeks, but in April 1965 he was called up to the senior England squad for a three-match tour of Yugoslavia, West Germany and Sweden. He could not dislodge George Cohen or Ray Wilson from either of the full-back slots during the tour and had to wait longer to win his first cap. Nonetheless, the exposure that linking up with the England set-up brought may have played a part in Keith beginning to be linked in the press with more wealthy rival clubs. Bill Nicholson's Tottenham Hotspur was reported to be one club monitoring the defender.

International honours would finally come, in the left-back position, against West Germany, on 23 February 1966. Alf Ramsey tinkered with his line up, looking at options as that summer's World Cup finals approached. Keith's 'England jinx' appeared to strike again when, on 43 minutes, he collapsed in agony on the slippery Wembley turf, having wrenched a knee in a collision with Gordon Banks. X-rays taken in London confirmed the extent of the injury as severe bruising rather than something more lasting, and he was soon back playing for his, by then, struggling club.

With Ray Wilson injured in FA Cup action for Everton, Ramsey gave Keith the nod again for the subsequent international fixture on 2 April - against the 'Auld Enemy' at Hampden Park. Keith was playing golf at Pleasington when Jack Marshall got word from Alf Ramsey of the call-up. The Rovers manager rang Barbara who left a message at the clubhouse to be passed to Keith on completion of his round. He was pleasantly surprised: 'I couldn't believe it at first. Had it been April 1, I would have suspected a leg-pull. But it is great news, and I am looking forward to my first experience of the Hampden roar I've heard so much about.' Keith flew up to Scotland, to join the squad training camp at Troon. Before a mind-bogglingly large crowd of 123,000, Keith was giving a testing afternoon by Celtic's Jimmy Johnstone, but the visitors edged the match 4-3.

A month later, Ray Wilson was restored to the England team, wearing the number three shirt when England took on Yugoslavia but, two days later, Keith was included in the 28-man group selected by Alf Ramsey to train at the FA's

Keith and Jack Charlton in defensive action for England against Scotland in 1966

facility in Lilleshall, Shropshire (it soon become 27 in the group when Everton's Brian Labone chose to drop out due to his pending nuptials). When interviewed in the spring, Keith had disclosed that he and Barbara had held off booking a summer holiday: 'I am not even thinking of holidays this year. I'm just hoping against hope that I'll be with the England party. That's my great ambition.'

It was not to be, however. With Ray Wilson overcoming a debilitating back-problem and George Cohen recovering from a leg injury, Alf Ramsey felt able to omit the Blackburn Rovers man from the final squad of 22. Cover for Cohen and Wilson would be provided by Jimmy Armfield of Blackpool and Liverpool's Gerry Byrne (who, like Keith, had just two full caps to his name). The other unfortunates to be sent home from Lilleshall in mid-June (but told to keep fit and available, just in case) were Liverpool pair Gordon Milne and Peter Thompson, Chelsea's Bobby Tambling and Johnny Byrne of West Ham. It was a huge blow for Keith - the finals had come just too soon for him to truly establish himself at international level. It made him all the more determined to make the final cut four years later.

CHAPTER FOUR
UNSETTLING TIMES

On the domestic football front, Blackburn's so-called Marshall's Misfits (a reference to many of the players thriving, having been slotted into unfamiliar positions) had threatened to challenge for silverware. The established international players like Bryan Douglas, Ronnie Clayton and Michael McGrath were now joined in the side by Keith, Mike England, John Byrom, Mike Ferguson, Andy McAvoy and Fred Pickering. Thumping West Ham United 8-2 on Boxing Day 1963, they found themselves at the pinnacle of the table. However, form then became erratic – in spite of Fred Pickering's outstanding forward partnership with Andy McAvoy (a player likened to Jimmy Greaves for his cool finishing). The team slid to a disappointing 7th place finish.

Keith's absence from mid-February through injury sustained at the England training camp was a major factor as was the sale of Fred Pickering to Everton in early March. Local lad John Byrom replaced Pickering in the Rovers team - and did so with aplomb. A mid-table finish in 1964/65 season - in which Keith alternated frequently between the two full-back positions (and even appeared in the half-back and forward lines when circumstances necessitated it) – was creditable. However, just one win in the final seven fixtures was an omen of tougher times ahead.

The 1965/66 season started in difficult circumstances, with the town in the grip of a polio epidemic. With the first cases of the disease reported in early

The so-called Marshall's Misfits - the Blackburn Rovers 1963-64 team

March 1965 - Celebrating a Rovers goal with John Byrom in a defeat of West Ham

August, Rovers were obliged to do their pre-season training in the safety of the Netherlands, and several early-season matches were postponed. Attendances at Ewood were impacted by the outbreak as a local doctor advised: 'Stay by the fireside and watch TV - it's safer.'

The team, without the craft of knee injury-plagued Bryan Douglas for much of the season, was playing catch-up without ever achieving it. The previously prolific strike-force – perhaps missing the creativity of Douglas, hit a barren run. Andy McAvoy and John Byrom only managed 13 goals between them. In stark contrast, the club's FA Cup form was impressive, with Rovers picking off Arsenal and West Ham. With a fixture back-log piling up, Rovers were hindered by the absence of Keith in some matches (because of the injury sustained in his full international debut) and lost all but one of 13 games in the season's run-in. It culminated in the humiliation of a rock-bottom finish; a meagre 20 points having been picked-up (13 shy of Northampton Town in 21st position). The club directors claimed that Rovers would be promoted within a year of relegation. In the event, it was a quarter-century wait, ended by the largesse and vision of Jack Walker.

Unsurprisingly, the vultures hovered above Ewood in the summer of 1966, ready to pick off Rovers' best players. The relegation (and the subsequent failure to make a quick return to top-flight football) was a source of considerable frustration for Keith. Once the club's fate was sealed in the spring of 1966, he submitted a transfer request. Barbara explained the situation in the local newspaper, acknowledging that her husband might come in for some flak: 'Keith wants to get on in football and he's been talking to me about trying to get a transfer for some time. People are going to knock Keith, just as they knocked Fred Pickering when he decided that he wanted to better himself and leave Blackburn.' There was speculation about a £40,000 bid from Liverpool, with Bill Shankly reported to be very keen to add the full-back to the reigning champions' squad. Two big-name departures were Mike England to Spurs and John Byrom who was surprisingly allowed to join Bolton. Roverite reaction to a further big-name exit would have been cataclysmic, so the club was firm in its stance that it would trigger a two-year extension option on Keith's contract, which was on the verge of expiring.

After further transfer speculation, some of it fueled by Keith himself, Rovers persuaded the full-back to shelve a transfer request and sign a new contract. The six-year agreement (three years with the option of three more) was signed around the time of the birth of son Craig, in December 1967. Barbara explained to the press: 'Keith was unsettled but we decided that rather than move for a bigger pay packet, we preferred to stay here with our friends and neighbours.' Although the new contract - generous by Rovers standards but some way below big club top-flight packages - brought more security and continuity, it meant Keith faced life away from the pinnacle of club football and the 'shop window' for international selection.

With the ink barely dry on the contract paperwork, the 26-year-old har-boured doubts about the wisdom of having committed himself for so long. In the wake of his finest England performance to date - at right-back in place of the injured George Cohen in a European Championship match at Hampden Park on 24th February 1968 - he gave a remarkably candid Sunday newspaper interview to James Mossop. Keith confessed, 'Since I got back from Glasgow last weekend, I have talked for ages with my wife about the future. In many ways it seemed a great thing, at the time, so I signed the contract. Now I am definitely having regrets...I like living in the town, but this weekend has really set me think-ing.' This disclosure must have induced convulsions in the Ewood Park corridors of power. A £100 fine - a week's wages – was passed down to Keith for going public with his thoughts.

He would continue to be linked with moves to several top-flight clubs. After an emergency board meeting, in March 1968, Rovers transfer listed the full-back. Frustrated supporters, fearing the exit of another of Ewood's jewels, daubed the exterior wall of the Nuttall Street stand with the messages: 'Pickering, England – not Newton' and 'Sack the board'. The Newtons, meanwhile, received anon-ymous letters accusing Keith of disloyalty to the club. Barbara felt moved to appeal, via the local press, for the letters to stop – pointing out that the board had put her husband on the transfer list.

The news of the transfer-listing sparked a scramble for the international full-back's signature. With Sheffield Wednesday preparing a bid, Nottingham Forest stole a march. Johnny Carey and his Nottingham Forest chairman, Tony Wood, sped up from the Midlands in Woods' Rolls Royce to try to conclude a deal valued at in the region of £90,000. They met Keith and Rover's chairman Douglas Hull at Ewood Park for talks. Terms were agreed but Keith asked for the opportunity to discuss matters with Barbara before reaching a final decision. The couple concluded that they did not wish to uproot themselves from Lancashire so the deal was the off.

In spite of the sometimes-strained relationship with the board, Keith continued to deliver the goods where it counted - on the pitch, thus keeping at bay the challenge of Gary Coxon, a full-back signed from Everton. For Coxon, the task of trying to dislodge the England international from the team was a thankless one: 'I was his understudy – the trouble was that Keith never got ill and never got injured! He was like lightning – such a quick full-back. He was very much a family man and not one for going out much. Later, I would meet up with him occasionally when holidaying in Abersoch, where we'd bump into him and Barbara on the beach.'

Billy Wilson had become the Rovers left-back during the relegation season and established himself thereafter - with Keith operating at right-back. Eddie Quigley, the former Rovers forward who had returned to the town as manager in the spring of 1967, was quoted as saying: 'Young Billy Wilson has become a better playing because he is partnering Keith. The Newton skills and his completely professional approach to the game are rubbing off on Billy.'

Club historian Harry Berry eulogises about this defensive partnership which lasted for four years: 'Wilson was a hell of a player and with Keith he formed the best full-back pairing that Rovers have ever had. It was hard work playing against them. In those days wingers swapped over if they were not getting much joy - but Keith and Billy each tackled equally hard! Keith was a tremendous player, like a force of nature. When he drove forward, he would get forward 50 yards with no trouble. He was a really hard guy, and he had that way of running with the ball that made people reluctant to challenge him.'

Keith's consistent excellence at club level, even in the Second Division, meant that Alf Ramsey had no qualms about selecting him as the first choice right-back from 1968 onwards, in succession to George Cohen. Keith had won Ramsey's trust, not only through his ability but his honesty. Barbara told journalist Tom Holden about a match against Ireland when Keith had failed to win the ball in the air before the opposition scored: 'At the end of the game Ramsay asked Keith what happened, and he just said, "It was all my fault." And Ramsay [then] told him he was playing on Saturday. He was testing him to see if he had the bottle to own up. He knew in that instant that if he made excuses, he'd be dropped.'

Eddie Quigley sometimes deployed his star defender in a more advanced, midfield, position, explaining: 'Playing Keith Newton at full-back is rather like having a Rolls Royce and using it only at weekends. His talents would be best used in midfield where he could control a game…but for us to use him in this way would jeopardise his England chances. As it is, he doesn't merely play old-fashioned full-back for us. He uses his skills as they are called on – breaking when necessary, tying up the opposition when necessary.' Two seasons in the upper reaches of the second tier of English football were followed by a disappointing 1968/69 campaign. The England curse struck again when Keith injured a thigh playing at Wembley against Bulgaria in early December. Barring one FA Cup appearance, he was out of the team until late February 1969, even doing a spot of Russian dancing exercises to aid his recovery (this provided a great photo opportunity for the local press – son Craig also being roped in). His return did not reverse the abject form of the team - which registered just one League win after January. Losing the final six matches of the season, Rovers finished just two positions above the drop zone to the Third Division. Keith was no closer to a return to the top flight and he feared for his England prospects. The end of the season also saw two Rovers legends, and Keith's fellow England internationals, bring the curtain down on their professional careers. Ronnie Clayton and Bryan Douglas played their last matches in the blue and white halves in April. It was the end of an era at Ewood.

CHAPTER FIVE
THE TOFFEE

Although Eddie Quigley down-played the possibility of the right-back's exit, a £100,000 tag was slapped on the player when he submitted a fresh transfer request in the summer of 1969. Newspaper reports hinted that it would be Manchester United or Everton in pole position to acquire his services.

Keith would later confess that, at this time, he was hoping high-flying Everton would be the club to make a move for him. Certainly, the Toffees, with a brand of slick, attacking football, seemed like a natural fit for the accomplished full-back. The Merseysiders had lost the world-class left-back Ray Wilson in the summer of 1969, following a knee injury that hampered his pace and mobility. However, any desire of the one-time Mersey Millionaires to acquire Keith's services was quelled by Rovers' asking price. With no incoming transfer ensuing, it fell to the ever-dependable Sandy Brown to don the number three shirt for the first half of the 1969/70 season - in which the Toffees were determined to have a tilt at the title.

Speculation would continue about Keith's footballing future and the press would even follow the Newtons, with their young son Craig, on their holiday getaway to Guernsey, hoping to get a scoop. Southampton would agree a fee with Rovers in late September, and the Saints boss Ted Bates flew up to try to talk Keith into moving to the south coast. Bates was persuasive, but in the end Keith and Barbara's desire to remain in Lancashire put paid to the deal being agreed.

The Newton family during the 1969/70 season

Rover's strong start to the 1969/70 season, and other changes at the club, saw Keith coming round to the idea of coming off the transfer list. He told Joe Melling: 'When I asked for a transfer, I had become really fed-up with Second Division football and the club in general. I just couldn't wait to get away to make a fresh start. But things have changed at Ewood since then. There is a new atmosphere at the club and a real will-to-win spirit...Also the training and coaching at the club has radically changed.' However, Everton's Merseyside derby defeat on 6 December set in train the end of Keith's time with Rovers.

Everton supremo Harry Catterick, all too aware of the mounting challenge from Leeds United in the title race, decided to intensify his pursuit of the Blackburn man, and a fee in the region of £80,000 was agreed between the clubs. Although not well-publicised at the time, Rovers had a cash flow issue and could not turn down the offer. Keith had been thinking that any chance of a move to Goodison had faded and was on the point of withdrawing his transfer request, when things suddenly fell into place. He had recovered from a broken bone in his foot and returned to first team duties on Saturday 13 December. Two days later, on the second birthday of his son, the full-back reported for training, only to be told that a deal had been agreed with Everton and he would be driving over with Johnny Carey to Liverpool to meet Catterick and complete the transfer paperwork (the Irishman had returned to Rovers in January 1969 as Administrative Manager, with Eddie Quigley concentrating purely on team matters).

Arriving at Bellefield - Everton's training centre - for talks, Keith made one stipulation to the Toffees' manager: he would only sign if he was permitted to continue residing in Blackburn. Although he preferred players to live in the environs of Liverpool, on this occasion Harry Catterick did not demur – so keen was he to get the deal over the line. With the ink drying on the paperwork, Messrs. Newton, Catterick and Carey were photographed together by the press. Then the Everton manager and his new signing posed, slightly awkwardly with bats in hand, at a table tennis table. Mike Charters, the *Liverpool Echo's* sportswriter, whetted Evertonians' appetites when describing the big-money capture: 'Everton fans will recognise quickly that he is a defender in the classic mould, always aiming to make good, constructive, use of the ball.'

Reports of the transfer give clear evidence that Keith felt conflicted by the move away from Ewood Park. He'd wanted to test himself at a higher level – and bolster his chances of selection for England's travelling party to Mexico - by returning to the First Division. But he also felt a great affinity towards his adopted home-town. For Barbara, too, there were mixed emotions to contend with, as she told the *Liverpool Echo*: 'Keith phoned me up from Ewood Park yesterday morning and said that he was going to Everton for talks. It was a shock. I have very mixed feelings about the transfer. I'm glad for Keith, he has got into the First Division, but we'll miss him at Rovers. He has been with them for 11 years. I honestly thought that he'd finish his career with them. You should have seen his face when he came home last night. He had been down to the Park to collect his boots for the last time. He was really down in the mouth.'

The news of Keith's exit was met with dismay in the Lancashire mill town. Roverites bemoaned the impact it would have on their promotion chances (they were proved right as Rovers slipped from the top to finish the season in eighth place - six points off promoted Blackpool, who had Fred Pickering leading the line). It was a déjà vu situation for the dejected Ewood faithful, who had seen Roy Vernon and Fred Pickering lured to the same Merseyside club. Interviewed a few days later, Johnny Carey puffed his pipe as he told journalist Stan Liversedge that Keith had pushed for the move - true to an extent but neglecting to mention Blackburn's financial concerns: 'Primarily the reason for the transfer was that Keith wanted to leave. He had asked to go more than once…' When pushed by the interviewer about the financial reasons behind Rover's willingness to sell, Carey replied: 'We have a tremendous bonus scheme - £15 a point until we have collected 35 points, then the bonus shoots up.' At this time Rovers were on 33 points, so the tacit implication was that Rovers could ill-afford to pay the bonuses without a player sale-derived cash injection.

At Bellefield there were familiar faces from England duty to help Keith feel at home in Alan Ball, Brian Labone, Tommy Wright and Gordon West. Joe Royle, the Everton centre-forward, was very taken with his new club-mate: 'Keith was a really nice man who was totally unaffected by his status and never gave the kids a hard time. He was terrific on the ball and would be rated even higher if he played now. It was an anomaly that Tommy Wright was ranking ahead of him at right-back for Everton, but Keith was ranked in front of Tommy at right-back for England.' Keith would be billeted with John Morrissey for away matches - they got on well, but Keith would admit to losing sleep due to the winger's incessant snoring: 'I'd be knackered from lack of sleep, which wasn't exactly good preparation for a big match. Poor old Johnny did his best to cure the problem, he even tried taking tablets, but whatever he did couldn't cure his snoring! I just had to live with it.' The new man would strike up a strong bond with Howard Kendall and Alan Ball, after training they would often meet for a bite to eat in a Knotty Ash café.

The defender went straight into the team at right-back, at White Hart Lane on 17 December 1969, in place of the injured Tommy Wright. The watching Mike Charters confirmed that he looked a 'class player', adding that he was 'moving up smoothly into attack and distributing the ball well.' However, this debut was scrubbed from the record books when it was abandoned after just 30 minutes of play due to a floodlighting failure. After this aborted showing, the

Keith agonises about going close for Everton on his Goodison Park debut in December 1969

Toffees chairman, Jack Sharp, stated that the new man was clearly 'worth every penny' of the hefty fee, but Harry Catterick was more cautious in his assessment: 'We must wait and see how he gets on when he has a winger coming at him'. So, Keith's 'official' debut, came three days after the Spurs blackout debacle, with the visit of Derby County to a snow carpeted Goodison. With Tommy Wright fit again, Keith took Sandy Brown's place on the left side of defence. It was a solid outing, in which Keith nearly scored with a header, in a hard-fought 1-0 victory over the high-flying East Midlanders. In subsequent matches Keith was not at his best, looking fallible in defence - maybe a reaction to the unfamiliar surroundings, teammates and tactical system. In the eight games after the defeat of the Rams, Everton won just twice - a low point being dumped out of the FA Cup by Sheffield United. With the challenge for the title faltering due to this poor run of form, Everton fans were not slow to vent their anger. Keith – seen as a big-money arrival and expected to deliver polished performances – was on the receiving end of more than his fair share of terrace criticism. The discerning Evertonians measured him against the highest possible benchmark in Ray Wilson. In those early weeks of his Everton career, Keith would have benefitted greatly from having from the nous and industry of Colin Harvey in front of him, but the home-grown midfielder was absent with an eye complaint.

Subsequently, matters turned around for the team – and this was mirrored in Keith's own performances, which were increasingly impressive and more reminiscent of his best Ewood Park form. He told the *Echo*, 'There is no doubt that I feel a lot more confident now. I know I had a bad game or two with Everton, but I managed to get over it. Now I get the benefit of playing with top class men the whole time at the top of the First Division.' Meanwhile, Harry Catterick commented: 'Keith didn't play well in his first three or four games. Since then, he has steadily found his feet and got to know our style of play.' Mike Charters concurred: 'There are signs that he is beginning to find his feet in the Everton set-up… he is starting to look the part. It has taken him two months to settle down and clearly he has been instructed to tighten up his close marking and tackling.'

Upon joining the Blues, Keith briefly had a regular column in the *Liverpool Echo*. He used it to explain the step up in level he'd experienced at Goodison, and how it was spurring him on to raise his game: 'I had in my appetite whetted for the big time, through playing for England in front of crowds of up to 100,000. You anticipate such an occasion eagerly; you want to prove that you're one of the best. And when you go back to play in front of sparsely-populated terraces, you feel a sense of let-down. After the lord mayor's show, and all that. You begin to feel complacent, too. That after the heady business of pitting your wits and your skills against world-class players, you can cope with bread-and-butter Second Division fare well enough. I really believe that, subconsciously, you tend to take things more easily, and that you lose the fine edge from your play. But ever since I joined Everton, I have had that tingle of excitement, before every game. The crowd at Goodison is terrific, and you realise, even when you're playing away, that the fans look upon your team as something extra special. So, you have the incentive, every time, to show you are in the top class, as a professional footballer. Blackburn have my gratitude, because it was with them that I became an international. But I honestly believe that Everton offer me so much more opportunity to become a better player.'

On 11 March, the revitalised Toffees travelled down to White Hart Lane for another attempt at playing Spurs. It was foul weather, rather than floodlighting faults, which threatened the match on this occasion. Supporter Frank Keegan recalls: 'I travelled down wondering if the game would actually be played. Torrential rain throughout the day had put the game in doubt right up to kick off. With the pitch a quagmire, the game was decided by a single goal set up by Keith and finished brilliantly by Alan Whittle. This was perhaps Keith's finest performance in a blue shirt.'

Frank Keegan's praise is bittersweet as, on his 13th Everton appearance (and his first at right-back, if the curtailed Spurs match in December is discounted), Keith sustained a hamstring injury late in the game on that soggy pitch. After several days of rest in a nursing home, there were hopes that the injury might settle down and permit a return to action within a fortnight. The optimism was mis-placed. He would miss the final seven matches of the season, ceding his place to Sandy Brown. When the Blues sealed the Football League title on a cold April Fools' Day evening, Keith was pictured wearing a thick sheepskin coat, stood with the triumphant squad but somehow giving the impression of being apart. Maybe, his limited contribution due to a mid-season arrival at the club, and missing the run-in through injury, made him feel that he did not merit his winner's medal as much as the others.

CHAPTER SIX
MEXICO '70

Keith was sufficiently recovered to link up with the England squad in mid-April for the pre-World Cup friendly against Wales; he was selected at right-back for the subsequent match against Scotland at Hampden Park. He'd be one of four Everton players – alongside Alan Ball, Brian Labone (who'd also missed the title run-in through injury) and Tommy Wright - selected for the travelling party bound for the World Cup finals in Mexico. Goalkeeper Gordon West might have been there too, had he not declared himself unavailable due to domestic reasons. The Everton quartet received promotional cars from Ford and donned tuxedos to be filmed with the rest of the England squad singing *Back Home* before jetting off to the Americas.

His roommate on the trip was, as always on international duty, Bobby Charlton. The pair got on well and, from the off, Charlton had suggested that they room together. With only limited wardrobes for their eight-week stay in Central America, the pair they would swap jackets when going out for meals in order to mix things up a bit. Due to the exorbitant costs of inter-continental calls, they would take it in turns to phone home and pass messages on for the roommate's family. In subsequent years, Bobby would invite the Newton family to attend matches at Old Trafford. While the tournament was going on 2,000 miles away, Barbara would frequently answer her front door to find local kids on the step asking if she had any Keith Newton Esso World Cup coins that she could swap with others that they held.

Keith gives it some gusto as the England squad sings 'Back Home'

Refuelling during preparations for Mexico '70

Having featured in the warm-up matches staged in Bogotá and Quito, Keith was selected for the right-back berth when England's tournament got underway in Guadalajara on 2 June. He had a typically buccaneering first half against Romania, but his match came to a crashing halt in the heat of the Jalisco stadium. Shortly after half-time he took a kick to his kneecap in the latest in a series of late challenges from 'hatchet man' Mikai Mocanu. He recalled: 'I thought my leg had snapped. My eyes watered like they have never done before. You think all thoughts of terrible things when you go down like that. Ligament? Break? Was it the end of the tournament for me?' Barbara, watching at home in Blackburn, confessed to shouting at her TV when her husband was sent crashing to the turf. She told a reporter: 'That Rumanian player who fouled Keith got away with murder. He clobbered Keith's substitute as soon as he came on. Still, I'm glad England won.'

Club-mate Tommy Wright came on as substitute whilst Keith grimaced, fearing the worst. However, the damage to the knee proved to be no more than severe bruising. Wright played well in the defeat by Brazil five days later, but Keith was fit enough to resume his right-back duties when England defeated Czechoslovakia, nine days after sustaining his injury. Just three days later came the infamous quarter-final in Estadio de Guanajuato, León, against West Germany.

The reigning champions cruised into a two-goal lead with Keith integral to both goals. He delivered the low cross for Alan Mullery to open the scoring and repeated the feat in the second half for Martin Peters to slot home at the far post. However, in the energy-sapping midday heat in León, with Bobby Charlton brought off, England were rocked by goals from Beckanbauer and Seeler. Then, in extra time, Terry Cooper was beaten on England's left flank, Keith was out-jumped from the resultant cross and Gerd Müller volleyed home from close range. England were out.

In the aftermath, Alf Ramsey gathered the dejected squad at the hotel poolside. Joining them in a drink, the manager stated that it was the strongest England squad that he'd ever managed. Keith had had an excellent tournament yet, although at his peak, he would never add to his tally of 27 caps. Ramsey, perhaps seeking a fresh start, selected Peter Storey, Paul Reaney and Paul Madeley to share the right-back duties for the national side. In spite of this, Keith would never have a bad word said against his former national team manager.

CHAPTER SEVEN
IN THE SHADOWS

Back home, Keith and his fellow fatigued England and Everton club-mates prepared for the defence of the League crown. Many pundits predicted years of dominance ahead for the Toffees. The optimism was lent credence by a comfortable 2-1 victory in the season's Charity Shield curtain-raiser at Stamford Bridge. Keith, himself, appeared ready to put a difficult first half-season at Everton, on a personal level, behind him and show supporters his true ability: 'When I joined Everton, it was the first time I had played left-back for a long time. I was getting acclimatised to the position and getting on quite well when I got injured. I have the confidence back, which I seemed to miss when I went to Everton. Coming straight from Blackburn, and not knowing anybody at Everton, I felt a bit lonely at first. Training and playing in Mexico has helped me regain my fitness after that hamstring injury last season.'

However, once the League season got underway, the Toffees appeared to be stuck in their starting blocks - not registering a win until the seventh match of the season. A sign that giving Alan Ball the club captaincy on a permanent basis, after deputising for Brian Labone, was an error of judgement came in the fourth match of the season. The Toffees travelled to Leeds for a match to be captured for posterity by the TV cameras. Everton conceded a sloppy goal in a 3-2 defeat, when a poor pass from Brian Labone captured Keith flat-footed and let in Leeds for an equaliser. In the immediate aftermath, simmering tensions bubbled to the

Everton - The Champions, 1970

surface as Alan Ball went to remonstrate with his former England colleague and heated words were exchanged. Mike Chaters, in his report for the *Liverpool Echo*, described the 'rumpus': 'Ball, the new Everton captain, could be seen telling Newton what he thought about it in an angry outburst of words. Newton replied and the incident looked as though it was going to develop beyond words until Brian Labone pushed Newton to one side and Joy Royle did the same with Ball. The confrontation lasted only a few moments but few in the 46,718-crowd missed it.'

Ball was quoted afterwards in the *Echo*: 'We did have a go on the pitch, but it is better to do this than just walk away and forget it. Keith agrees that it is the best to get such things off your chest.' In *Everton Greats: Where Are They Now?* Keith gave a different take to his teammate on the incident: 'Bally came racing back to have a right go at the defence. We just felt that was totally uncalled for, and that he was better occupied getting back up the pitch and doing his own job.'

The League season was a miserable one for the reigning champions, culminating in a 14th place finish. The reasons for the mysterious collapse in form have been dissected elsewhere. Reasons cited include post-Mexico fatigue of key players, staleness in the team, injuries, imprudent transfer activity and even a degree of complacency. Progress in the European Cup and the FA Cup gave some grounds for positivity, however. In spite of the team's woes, Keith had been an ever-present that season, attaining a good level of consistency until succumbing to a knee injury near the end of normal time in the epic match against Borussia Monchengladbach (Everton winning in the penalty shoot-out with Keith's replacement, Sandy Brown, being one of the scorers).

His absence would see his namesake Henry Newton – a big-money signing from Nottingham Forest to bolster Everton's midfield options – deputising at left-back. In January, a frustrated Keith, who had not been recalled after being declared fit again, held what the press described as 'clear the air talks' with Harry Catterick. It was made clear by the manager that the club would not be transfer listing him: 'There is nothing like competition for keeping a player on top form. I expect every player to be keen to win back his place. I would be disappointed if Keith was not disappointed about being left out.' On a happier note, Keith returned to Ewood Park in December 1970, pulling on a 'Great Britain' select XI jersey, alongside Mike England, Bobby Moore and Geoff Hurst, for Ronnie Clayton's testimonial match.   In the early months of 1971, Keith would make sporadic first team appearances - including in the two ill-fated European Cup quarter-final legs against Panathinaikos and the gut-wrenching FA Cup semi-final defeat to Liverpool (his last appearance of the season). He'd been playing through the pain barrier with a groin injury (as was Alan Ball), which compromised his performances. He would later explain: 'I did have problems with various injuries. But the real trouble was that Harry never believed me. I could be literally hobbling around, unable to walk, and still, he wouldn't believe me. It was strange.' With the groin injury worsening, he was finally rested and then relegated to reserve team duties.

The first of several transfer requests followed as the relationship between player and manager became increasingly strained. Although the Everton supremo had built a side based on pure footballing principles in the late 1960s, he was insistent that the Mancunian full-back should curb his attacking sensibilities, focus on defence and not tarry so much on the ball before offloading it. Maybe this was a reaction to the team's indifferent form in the 1970/71 season and a desire for a back-to-basics approach by the back four. In subsequent years Keith was frank about his differences with Catterick: 'I have always been regarded as a creative type of player...and Catterick felt I tried to be too creative...When we were under pressure away from home, for example, Catterick generally expected the Everton defenders to hit long balls upfield for centre-forward Joe Royle to chase. My tendency to try and play my way out of trouble led to a certain amount of friction. I have long felt strongly that defenders should be able to express themselves on the field, like midfielders and forwards. That's precisely why Ajax are the number one team in Europe.'

In the end a bemused Keith asked Catterick, 'Why did you sign me?' It is still a head-scratcher as to how the Everton manager – normally a studious assessor of potential signings - ended up signing a full-back that he never seemed to have full confidence in. Catterick, who never went on record to explain his differences with the full-back, did tend to favour players who would give unquestioning, and unstinting, effort rather than the more cerebral and independently minded types who might offer a different viewpoint. Keith, like Alex Young, probably fell into the latter category, which was sometimes viewed with suspicion by the manager. In fairness to Catterick, Keith did struggle to replicate his Rovers form at Everton. There are several likely contributing factors to this: stepping back up to the top flight after three years in the Second Division, injuries, playing in a team whose form had collapsed, unfamiliar tactics or difficulty in adapting to (with due respect to Blackburn Rovers) a bigger club with all of the associated pressures and expectations. Keeping his home in Blackburn rather than relocating to Merseyside may also have hindered his assimilation at the club.

When asked to explain why Everton had not kicked on after the 1970 title win, Keith offered these thoughts: 'I feel that the side should never have collapsed as it did with the players they had available. I felt that the team was over-trained at times, everything was done to the stopwatch.' In another post-Everton interview, the Burnley man would refer to Bellefield as having a Colditz-like ambiance and intimated that squad spirit was compromised by sniping between players

Keith at Everton in 1970

Keith challenges John Hollins of Chelsea

over their indifferent form. By the end of the 1970/71 season both of Everton's Newtons were reportedly unhappy: Keith because he wasn't playing at left-back - and Henry because he was.

A malaise was enveloping the club by the time the 1971/72 season got under-way, but at least Keith was back in favour, making 15 consecutive appearances. However, another 3-2 defeat at Elland Road sounded the death knell for his time with the Blues. In the wake of the defeat, in which Everton had given a reason-able performance, the full-back was dropped from the side. The acquisition of little-known Falkirk defender John McLaughlin was a clear signal from Harry Catterick that Keith would not occupy the left-back position in the long-term. The lightweight and prematurely balding Scot - who Catterick likened to former player Warney Cresswell in appearance - was surprisingly tigerish in the tackle (earning him his 'big cat' nickname) but, in honesty, was nowhere near to being in Keith's footballing class. Even the injury woes of Tommy Wright - who would be forced to retire in 1973 - did not offer Keith a way back into the team at right-back, the manager choosing to blood Peter Scott instead.

Alan Ball joined Keith in being surplus to requirements when, out of the blue, sold to Arsenal in December 1971. Years later, perhaps with the Elland Road rumble still in his mind, Keith was forthright about his brilliant but feisty former teammate: 'Alan was a fabulous player, but by the time he left he'd driven us all mad with his incessant moaning. He was really whinging at all of us. When he left the club, it wasn't a shock to any of us; it was almost a relief. Alan Ball wasn't very good for team morale.' Corroborating Keith's observations, this pas-sage in Howard Kendall's autobiography recounts the club captain's simmering frustration in a training session, just prior to his exit: 'You could tell Bally wasn't interested. He was sulking... He put his hands out and said, "How can I train with this lot?"' Languishing on the fringes of the team, Keith did little to endear him-self to his manager - who sought to keep a tight rein on comments to the media - by publicly voicing, on more than one occasion, his feelings of discontent. The dejected defender would make his final appearance for the Toffees when drafted into the team for a torrid defeat by Chelsea in late January 1972.

CHAPTER EIGHT

RHAPSODY IN
CLARET AND BLUE

Keith would tell the journalist Vince Wilson of his anguish in the final months of his time at Everton: 'After I was dropped and probably forgotten by the supporters, I felt embarrassment. I was still drawing more money than some players playing in the first team.' He was made available for transfer in late December 1971 - the day before the sale of Alan Ball. With his star seemingly on the wane, and Everton seeking a transfer fee, Keith attracted no serious offers from other clubs. As transfer deadline day approached in March 1972, with Keith's contract due to expire in the summer, Harry Catterick phoned and said, 'What am I going to do with you?' In response, the player told his manager to play him or let him move on.

When no transfer was sealed before the deadline, Keith saw out his Everton career in the shadows. He later reflected: 'I left Everton feeling that I hadn't done justice to myself and wasn't allowed to express myself in my play as I should have done. While things did not go right for me at Everton, and I was unfortunate that my style did not fit in with what Harry Catterick wanted, Everton were a great club as far as I am concerned.' His low-key Goodison departure was a crying shame for all parties. In two and a half seasons he played just 47 times for the Toffees. Frank Keegan sums it up: 'I always felt that Everton fans never got to see the best of Keith, who was a classy full back at the right club - but at the wrong time.'

It is to Harry Catterick and Everton's credit that Keith was granted a free transfer when his contract expired at the end of May. In those pre-Bosman Ruling days, clubs could still collect a transfer fee, even upon expiry of a player's contract. Burnley manager Jimmy Adamson had been monitoring the situation for some months and swiftly moved to sign Keith. It was a reprieve for Keith who had envisaged himself leaving the game: 'I became very despondent and felt that I was going to drift out of the game at the age of 30. I was ready to take a job in South Africa when Burnley came along.' The switch exceeded all expectations for the player and his new club. Three years into his time at Turf Moor he opened up to journalist Ann Cummings about the contrast between Everton and Burnley: 'We have fun here. The training is serious but with a lot of tomfoolery. At Burnley we believe in flair and attack and our ambition is to win something now to bring glory back to Burnley.'

As well as crediting Jimmy Adamson for the freedom given to Burnley players to express themselves, Keith also put much of the Clarets' resurgence down to the team spirit fostered through many of the players being products of the club's youth system. One such Turf Moor graduate, Martin Dobson, was greatly impressed by the old hand who helped steer the team to the Second Division title in his first season back in East Lancashire: 'The 1971/72 season had been up and down - we won the last six or eight games but did not get promotion. So, Jimmy - who was a wonderful coach - looked for a senior player and must have done his homework on Keith. As soon as he came into the dressing room, he got that respect; here was an England World Cup player with knowledge of the game. It was a masterstroke by Adamson – seeing the quality in the guy. And it was not only as a footballer – it was the way he talked to the young lads, who needed that guidance. He was great on the ball and had awareness and anticipation of danger – and he was so comfortable in possession. Jimmy wanted someone to play from the back – so we were always looking for the back four to bring it up. Keith played in nearly every game at left-back with young Nick Docherty at right back. That was the perfect scenario - the team was better, and we were in the top two or three all season and eventually became champions.'

Another new teammate was Geoff Nulty, who had joined the Clarets from

Stoke City in 1969. He shared his impressions of his Burnley teammate: 'I remember that when he came, he used to come in to training in the car he'd been given as part of the England squad for Mexico. The players thought, "Wow! This guy played in the World Cup." That defined that he was from a different level, as nobody else in the side had played for England, at that point. He was quiet - but he fitted in with everybody - as he remembered where he had first come from. He was a really top professional who I admired, and on the pitch he had a tremendous impact. He could play right-back or left-back and was never put under pressure by a winger. He was a wonderful passer of the ball with his right foot and left foot. Wherever he got the ball he never seemed flustered.'

Promotion was secured with four games in hand when the Clarets eased to victory over Sunderland. For Barbara Newton, watching the match from the Turf Moor stands, it was a proud moment: 'It was so exciting during the match, and we still feel a glow at the prospects of playing in the First Division again.'

Burnley players celebrate promotion in the bath at Deepdale, 1973

A 1-1 draw away to Preston on the ultimate day of the season confirmed the Lancastrians as champions, ahead of QPR. The players celebrated in the communal bath with a makeshift trophy. The genuine divisional trophy was presented a few days later at the testimonial match for John Angus. The jubilant team paraded the silverware around the Turf Moor pitch after the match.

Keith would reflect on the influence he had on the young players in the promotion season: 'I'm convinced that I gave more to my club last season than ever before. I offered the team experience, I slowed the lads down, stopped them racing about. Some of them were astounded to see me attending to my fingernails during the tense moments in games…but everything was designed for cool. I think I offered them more by example and illustration than I did with my tongue.'

Adamson, for his part, described Keith as a player who knew 'how to pass, when to pass and why to pass' and seasoned journalists hailed him as the finest Clarets full-back since John Angus. Richard Bott of the *Sunday Express* painted this picture with words: 'Keith Newton...a tall, bronzed athlete who brings an artist's touch and a vivid splash of colour to the defender's cold and ruthless role.' The admiration was a view shared by Burnley supporter Tony Scholes: 'I have been watching Burnley for 60 years now, and I would say that Keith Newton is one of our two best right-backs - and two best left-backs. I'd put him alongside John Angus and Alex Elder, who were our full backs when I was first watching. He was just a wonderful footballer - so cultured. I was talking to Colin Waldron about the Leeds team of that time, and he told me, "Every team had players who could go "over the top". We had our entire back four [who could] – except Keith Newton, because he was so good that he didn't need to do that." Any player that signs for Burnley who has previously played for Blackburn starts at "below zero" with the fans - so you have got to play well. And Keith just did.'

Craig Newton, by then of primary school age, was permitted to travel on the Clarets team coach to matches with his father and attended pre-season matches. In conversation with the journalist Tom Holden, he rekindled fond memories of that period: 'For me it was a fantastic time, I always had a massive grin on my face. I remember walking out onto the pitch at Turf Moor one pre-season and Paul Fletcher was there with the coach, running up and down the pitch. He said,

Parading the Second Division winner's trophy at Turf Moor

"Come on Craig, are you having a run with me?" So, there I was running up and down Turf Moor with Paul Fletcher in my shorts and trainers.' Craig also recalled a 1973 post-season holiday in Spain with family and a few of his father's teammates to celebrate promotion. "It was the end of the season, sangria on the beach and all that, but then these waiters found out these guys were from Burnley and had just won the Second Division title. So after about a week, these waiters challenged the players to a game. This game was on a sandy pitch at the back of the beach, and it was hilarious seeing these athletes, with six-packs and built shoulders, against these waiters who were running around like headless chickens. They didn't stand a chance, but they loved it. Despite being beaten terribly, the waiters talked about it all week and the players didn't have to leave their sunbeds the entire time. They had so much respect for them.'

The return to the top flight was preceded by the 1973 Charity Shield fixture, as Liverpool and Sunderland had chosen not to participate. In the match, staged

Burnley squad photo - 1975

at Maine Road, Burnley duly beat Manchester City by one goal to nil. The team quickly adapted to First Division football and was only denied qualification for the UEFA Cup on goal difference. A return to Goodison Park for a League encounter in October 1973 (a 1-0 win for the Toffees through a Dave Clements penalty) was an emotional moment for the resurgent full-back and vindication of the belief in his own ability. The club also reached the FA Cup semi-final at Hillsborough, going down to Newcastle United.

Craig was coming to the age where he could appreciate his father's performances on the pitch and his level of fame off it: 'Dad never changed; he was just down to earth, polite with everybody- he didn't have a bad bone in his body. But on the football pitch he was a different character - it was his job. If you were a winger, he'd hit you like a sledgehammer, but in the bar afterwards he was a different person - he'd shake your hand and buy you a pint. After the game all of a sudden all of these people would swarm round him – and he'd be having his picture taken with people and doing presentations – and I'd be thinking, "That's my dad."' Barbara has similar memories of the contrast between footballer and family man: 'The mild-mannered person I knew wasn't the person I watched. I don't think he ever lost his temper at home but on the football pitch it was different. He could be ruthless sometimes – he made me cringe.'

Peter Noble became Keith's roommate for away fixtures and one of his closest friends at Turf Moor. In 1998 he told the *Lancashire Telegraph* about his pal: 'He was an absolutely superb player who made defending look easy. We played in a Burnley side which had a lot of young players and Keith's experience and guidance contributed to some of them becoming big names. Burnley fans will remember the partnership struck up between him and Leighton James down the flanks.'

Burnley's excellent debut season in the top flight was followed with a mid-table finish in 1974/75 - this in spite of selling Martin Dobson to help fund the construction of a new stand. A personal highlight for Keith was the 1-0 defeat of Liverpool at Anfield in September. He'd write in a column a few days later: 'What a result! Nothing in my career can beat the way I felt when I came off the pitch...The victory provided me with that extra personal bit of pleasure. That's because, as a former Everton player, the Anfield crowd don't like me...I had to put up with taunts such as "What the hell have you come back for?" and other more insulting remarks. There's no more satisfying way to answer these jibes than by picking up a win. I have never seen a team work as hard as we did on Tuesday night, and I was proud to be part of it.'

On Boxing Day 1975, Keith reached the landmark of 500 career Football League and cup appearances. The subsequent match, away to Manchester United, was his 500th start (he had made one appearance as a substitute for Everton), so both teams formed a guard of honour as the veteran came onto the pitch and saluted the crowd. In the next Turf Moor match, the Burnley and Derby County players walked out together before kick-off and stood in the centre circle as Keith was presented with a cut-glass decanter and set of crystal glasses by the Clarets' Chairman Bob Lord.

Marking the milestone, he gave an interview to Keith McNee in which he confessed to having 'a lot of mileage on the clock' but revealed that any marginal loss in pace was more than compensated for by hard-earned experience. He finished by telling the reporter: 'I feel as fit as ever and am determined to keep on playing for a few years yet.' He was true to his word. As well as natural athleticism, dedication and football intelligence, some of Keith's longevity could be attributed to his ability to switch off from the pressures of professional football: 'Because I am an easy-going fellow, I find it easy to relax. Even on holiday I just

Keith acknowledges the players and crowd at Old Trafford before his 500th start in club football

sit in a chair for hours with a book. Perhaps that is why I have lasted so long.'

The Clarets' habit of cashing-in on young talented players, borne of financial necessity, had weakened the team. Out had gone the likes of Martin Dobson, Leighton James and Geoff Nulty, whilst in came experienced pros in the autumn of their careers. These included Mike Summerbee from Manchester City and Willie Morgan back for a second spell at Turf Moor after a period at Manchester United. The latter said of Keith: 'He was very fit and fast for a full-back; most were ugly and slow, but he was the opposite.'

Mike Summerbee, meanwhile, has nothing but fond memories of his England and Burnley teammate: 'I'd first come up against Keith when he played for Blackburn and Everton. Playing against him, I probably got stuck in a bit, but he just carried on playing! He was a top-quality player. When I first played for England in 1968, he helped me to feel at home in the squad. At Burnley we were coming towards the end of our careers together. Someone once asked me when I'd pack it in and I said, "When the linesman overtakes me!" But there was nothing that you could say against Keith as a player. He was outstanding – "Mr. Reliable". He could play left-back, right-back and centre-half. At Burnley when he went beyond me, I just picked him out with the ball as I knew that there was an end product there. He was ahead of his time in that way. It's alright having full-backs who can go forward from a defensive situation to being a winger - but he was the perfect crosser and could pick somebody out. On one occasion the centre-half was unavailable for a big game so Jimmy Adamson, the manager, said: "Keith will play centre-half and Mike, will you play left-back?" I had never played there in my life - but Keith spoke to me all the way through the game, telling me where to go and what do to. He was a quiet man, but he was funny with a dry sense of humour and we had some good times together socialising. Keith was a true professional, a gentleman and an exceptional player.'

With Burnley struggling in the League, Jimmy Adamson departed in January 1976 and was replaced by the first team coach Joe Brown. Willie Morgan, who had struggled with injury on his return to the club and departed for Bolton Wanderers shortly after Adamson's sacking, recalled: 'It was a good team, but things just didn't go right.' In the end Burnley were relegated on 28 points - six short of safety. Keith remained at the club and was awarded the captaincy upon the departure of Colin Waldron in the summer of 1976. In the build up to the next season he mused on why the team had been relegated: 'When you are in relegation trouble, the problem is that effort and enthusiasm take over from skill - and this is what happened to us. We have to get back to basics and find a blend. We have a good chance of making an impact in the Second Division.'

Things did not pan out as hoped - Burnley ended the 1976/77 season just two points clear of the relegation zone to the Third Division. Joe Brown was replaced by former manager Harry Potts before the end of the campaign. Keith had been relieved of the captaincy in favour of Peter Noble after half of the season. Perhaps the role of skipper - with the burdens it brought - did not sit well with him. In truth, Keith did not need the title of captain to be a positive and

Enjoying life at Burnley - with Barbara and Craig

calming influence on teammates.

In May 1978 - at the grand age of 36 - Keith finally brought down the curtain on his highly fulfilling spell at Turf Moor, in which he had rediscovered his love of the game and made 253 appearances. His final first team outing had come in February of that year - an away defeat to Brighton and Hove Albion. It brought his overall appearance tally in first class club football to 669. The veteran wasn't completely finished with football, however, as he spent the 1978/79 season with Northern Premier League outfit Morecambe FC. There followed a stint as player-manager of Clitheroe FC, but he soon decided that football management and playing at the lower level was not for him: 'I couldn't really adapt to the non-League level so decided to get out completely.'

He would disclose in *Everton Greats: Where Are They Now?* that he had hoped to get into coaching but found opportunities to be very limited: 'I applied for a number of coaching jobs, but always got the same reply: "Sorry, you haven't got enough experience." I'd have thought nearly 20 years playing top flight football, earning international caps and being in a championship-winning side would have been experience enough, but it wasn't what they were looking for. In the end I just gave up on getting into that side of football.'

Keith shows Craig some momentoes from his illustrious playing career

CHAPTER NINE
LIFE BEYOND FOOTBALL

Keith took on a newsagents shop near the junction of Richmond Terrace and Sudell Cross in central Blackburn. Football supporters would have the thrill of being served by this most unassuming of sports stars. Jim Standing, who would call in for his paper when working nearby, recalls that if the weather was clement, Keith would sit outside the shop, catching the sun's rays whilst enjoying a cigarette. A couple of years later he purchased the adjoining unit and opened a trophy business. He was always happy to oblige customers - including schools, boys clubs and local amateur sports teams - by coming down to present the trophies.

In his leisure time Keith was able to indulge in his passion for golf - playing every Saturday as a member of Wilpshire Golf Club. He'd be invited to take part in celebrity am-am tournaments, often taking son Craig along with him. His son was struck by the rapport his father had with fellow ex-footballers: 'The craic that they had - it was like they just picked up where they had left off in the changing room. There was that bond and respect – and for me it was unbelievable to watch.'

The shop work and golf limited opportunities to watch his former football teams. He was in the rare position of transcending the partisanship of Burnley and Blackburn Rovers but would confess to not being a good spectator: 'To be honest, I was always very bad at sitting and watching a game.' Nonetheless, he would occasionally go to Ewood Park with Barbara and Craig and catch up

with Ronnie Clayton, Bryan Douglas and their wives. He would also go over to
Wigan as a guest of Dave Whelan - who still referred to him, all those years later,
as Bunny. For Craig, being with his parents in the company of Clayton, Douglas
over dinner was a privilege: 'They were all close, and shared stories about when
they played for England and Rovers – I was hearing the true stories behind the
scenes. It was really nice to hear from three East Lancashire people – although
Dad was born in Manchester, he'd become a Blackburn man.'

A brief 'comeback' at Rovers came about in February 1980. Howard Kendall, a former teammate at Everton and, at this point, the Rovers player-manager,
invited Keith and Bryan Douglas to take part in training prior to the team's FA
Cup fifth round tie with Aston Villa. Keith and Bryan were photographed with
Kendall and Duncan McKenzie by the local paper - the former full-back still
looking fit enough to be playing the game. No doubt Kendall hoped that the experience of training alongside two former England internationals would inspire
his players. The plan almost worked - Rovers drew the match at Ewood Park but
lost in the replay by just one goal.

Subsequently, Keith was persuaded by an acquaintance to join the Fairways
car dealership in Preston, where he'd focus on commercial sales. His profile as
a sportsman helped to open the doors to businesses that might have remained
closed to others. By the 1990s he was working in business car sales at Lookers
in Blackburn. It was here that he met Everton historian David France for a chat
about his career. He recently reflected on their conversation for me: 'I recall that
he was immaculately attired – not one hair out of place. He was friendly and
chatted about his time at Everton and the 1970 World Cup. He said that - despite
winning the League and playing in the World Cup - in many ways Everton had
been the low point of his career, compared to the consistent form he enjoyed at
Blackburn and Burnley. What I remember most is that he complained about the
rigorous/demanding nature of the training routines at Bellefield. Too much running around the perimeter of the training ground and sprinting up and down the
pitch - not enough ball practice. He blamed the training for his delayed recovery
from injuries. Also, he felt that he never won over Gwladys Street supporters
– who were over-critical of the team when not winning. I recall that he was ex-

tremely impressed with Brian Labone, Howard Kendall, Colin Harvey and Joe Royle.'

The years of smoking cigarettes took their toll and Keith was diagnosed with lung cancer. Surgery in Blackpool, to remove a cancerous section of lung, necessitated removing a rib – replaced with a steel one. The procedure was initially deemed a success but, sadly, the cancer returned. After a short period at East Lancashire Hospice, Keith passed away on 16 June 1998 – a week shy of his 57th birthday.

When the sad news broke, flags flew at half-mast at Ewood Park and Turf Moor and tributes flooded in from around the football world. Ronnie Clayton, Keith's captain at Rovers, told the *Liverpool Echo*: 'It is a sad day for every club that Keith was associated with. He was a super guy, who remained a great friend of myself and Blackburn Rovers. Keith always looked a super footballer. He will be fondly remembered by Everton fans as a member of the magnificent 1970 championship-winning team. It is worth remembering that many of his finest performances came in the 1970 World Cup in Mexico.' Rovers' assistant manager at the time, Tony Parkes, told the *Lancashire Telegraph*: 'Keith was one of the new generation of very talented footballing full-backs who could play on either wing and his game wasn't just about being big and strong. He is a legend in the area and it's a tragedy to lose him.' Burnley and former Blackburn secretary John Howarth said: 'We were all very upset when we heard the news about Keith. He was a very nice gentleman, very well thought of and I've never heard anyone say a bad word about him. On the pitch he was an all-round class act, and he was something of an idol to me and many others.'

On Merseyside, Keith's Everton skipper, Brian Labone, paid his own tribute: 'Keith was a great player, both in our championship side and for England in Mexico – and he wasn't far behind Ray Wilson when you talk of great Everton full-backs. He was very, very quick and you would rarely see him lose his temper. He was a quiet man and it's very sad that anyone should die as young as he has.' Tommy Wright, another teammate for club and country, added to the outpouring of warmth, and expressed a hope that the FA would commemorate Keith's life and achievements in a forthcoming European Championship match: 'I was very sad to hear of Keith's death – it was a great shock to me. I think it would be nice if England wore black armbands for the Romania match, because Keith was such a nice, inoffensive kind of bloke who will be sorely missed. We had some great games together for Everton and England. He was a good player and always keen to go forward. I hope that the Football Association honours him in some way, because he deserves it.' In spite of the pleas from Tommy Wright and Ronnie Clayton, black armbands were not worn by the England team during the match against Romania on 22 June. The FA's public tribute was limited to the following statement: 'We extend our deepest sympathy to Mr. Newton's family and friends, and everyone connected with him.'

A funeral service was held six days after Keith's passing at St. Peter's parish church in Salesbury. It was followed by a cremation ceremony in Pleasington. The church was packed, with standing room only at the rear. Keith's former clubs were represented, and all sent floral tributes. The Burnley and Rovers chairmen, Frank Teasdale and Robert Coar, arrived at the church together; they joined the likes of Dave Whelan, Ronnie Clayton, Michael McGrath, Bryan Douglas, Peter Noble and Paul Fletcher in the congregation. Gordon Taylor, another former Rovers player, represented the PFA. Rev. John Hartley gave a glowing tribute in the eulogy. The cortège was given a police motorcycle escort as a mark of respect and the emotional occasion was covered on the regional TV news bulletin. It all served to confirm how popular this warm-hearted and easy-going man (off the football pitch, anyway) was.

Barbara is a regular match-goer at Ewood Park whilst Craig follows the fortunes of his dad's three former clubs: 'People ask me which team I support. I don't support any particular one, but I always want Blackburn, Everton and Burnley to do well, as dad played for them. Every Saturday I check to see how they have got on.' Keith's life ended far too soon, but he lives on in people's memories. People still stop Craig and Barbara to talk about him fondly and share anecdotes.

For Evertonians it is a source of regret that they didn't see the very best of him – and he didn't get to enjoy his time there as much as he'd have liked. Yet, he did earn a coveted League Championship medal and would reflect: 'There were problems at Everton, I will admit, but there were also some great times and great matches that I remember with fondness.' For supporters of Rovers and Burnley, they can look back on many years of service by this Rolls Royce of a defender, who helped to redefine the role of the full-back as the attacking force that we see in elite-level matches today.

Keith Newton 1941-1998

CAREER STATISTICS

Blackburn Rovers
(1960/61-1969/70)

League	306 (9)
FA Cup	21 (0)
League Cup	30 (1)
Total	357 (10)

Everton
(1969/70-1971/72)

League	48+1 sub (1)
FA Cup	2 (0)
League Cup	1 (0)
European Cup	6 (0)
Charity Shield	1 (0)
Total	58+1 (1)

Burnley
(1972/73-1977/78)

League	209 (5)
FA Cup	14 (1)
League Cup	14 (1)
Texaco Cup	7 (0)
Anglo Scottish Cup	6 (0)
Watney Cup	2 (0)
Charity Shield	1 (0)
Total	253 (7)

Morecambe *(1978/79)*

Clitheroe *(1980)*

England *(1966-1970)*

All competitions	27 (0)

Goals scored are shown in brackets

ACKNOWLEDGEMENTS

My sincere thanks to Barbara and Craig Newton for enabling me to tell Keith's story.

Alison and Peter Jones kindly proof-read the draft manuscript. Any errors remaining are mine alone.

Thanks to Thomas Regan of Milkyone Creative for design and typesetting

I am also indebted to Harry Berry, Gavin Buckland, Joyce Catterick, Brendan Connolly, James Corbett, Gary Coxon, Fred Cumpstey, Martin Dobson, Bryan Douglas, David Exall, Colin Harvey, David France, Tom Holden, Bernie Horne, John Hurst, Mike Jackman, Gary James, Steve Johnson, Frank Keegan, Vinnie and Rita Leech, Kathleen and Michael McGrath, Willie Morgan, Alan Miller, David Newton, Jean Newton, Geoff Nulty, George Orr, Mary Painter (Blackburn Library), Fred Pickering, Mike Royden, Joe Royle, John Roberts, Tony Scholes, Billy Smith, Jim Standing, Tony Sweet, Mike Summerbee, Mick Thexton, Spencer Vignes and 4000 Holes fanzine.

Finally, I appreciate the ongoing support of fellow members of the Everton FC Heritage Society.

If I have omitted anyone from these acknowledgements, I apologise.

Images are from the Newton family collection and are used with permission. The Reddish District Inter-League team image is used courtesy of Tony Sweet.

SOURCES

Books and articles

Blackburn Rovers: The Complete Record, Mike Jackman (Breedon Books)

Boys of 66: The Unseen Story Behind England's World Cup Glory, John Rowlinson (Virgin Books)

Everton: The Official Complete Record, Steve Johnson (deCoubertin)

Everton Greats: Where Are They Now? John Berman and Malcolm Dome (Mainstream)

Harry Catterick: The Untold Story of a Football Great, Rob Sawyer (deCoubertin)

Love Affairs & Marriage: My Life in Football, Howard Kendall with James Corbett (deCoubertin)

Money Can't Buy Us Love: Everton in the Sixties, Gavin Buckland (deCoubertin)

That Was My Dad, And He Played For England, Tom Holden (journ-web.shef.ac.uk)

The Everton Encyclopedia, James Corbett (deCoubertin)

The Men Who Made Blackburn Rovers FC Since 1945, Harry Berry (Tempus)

Obituary of Keith Newton in *The Independent* by Ivan Ponting

Newspapers and magazines

Daily Mirror, Lancashire Evening Telegraph/Lancashire Telegraph, Liverpool Daily Post, Liverpool Echo, Liverpool Football Echo, Shoot, Sunday Mirror/Sunday Express, The Independent

Websites

bluecorrespondent.co.uk

clarets-mad.co.uk

englandfootballonline.com

enfa.co.uk

evertonresults.com

findmypast.co.uk

theyflysohigh.co.uk

toffeeweb.com